Beir Bua

Press

www.BeirBuaPress.com

I'd Better Let You Go

Hold on to poetry !

by

Nikki Dudley

Published by Beir Bua Press

ISBN: 978-1-914972-01-0

Beir Bua Press, Co. Tipperary, Ireland.

Typesetting / Layout, Cover Layout: Michelle Moloney King

Cover image: Nikki Dudley

Ordering Information: For details, see www.BeirBuaPress.com

Published by Beir Bua Press

Printed in the UK

9 781914 972010

I'D BETTER LET YOU GO

NIKKI DUDLEY

for Greenie

Introduction

This collection is more personal than a lot of the stuff I normally write, at least overtly. My nan passed away in 2014 and for some reason, I finally felt ready to talk about it and of course, I did it via writing because it's the way I process the world.

There's a mixture of visual poetry, more lyrical poetry, creative non-fiction and hybrid forms in here. When I sat down to write about dementia, the chaos of forms felt kind of fitting. The mixture of styles felt right for me to explore such a challenging, confusing, and often heart-breaking condition. I couldn't help including some more experimental/visual work because I have a real passion for it but it also lent itself perfectly to the theme and the examination of a person's life, family and mind falling apart.

The fiction felt necessary to ground the pieces and pull everything together. While there's also some humour in there because despite everything, the shocks and oddities of dementia can be strangely humorous. In times of desperation and the unknown, humans have a tendency to try and find brightness, no matter where it comes from.

This collection is a dedication to my nan, who was one of my favourite people. I miss her all the time. So I had to write it out of me, to process the loss of her, in the best way I know.

STOP THE BUS

stopping the bus, don't ask me

to lose you like the light in autumn, steadily and slowly

feeling each tone. Then. /a curtain/

The bus is going on and on and oh, don't…

1947 will never be the same without you if you

swallow our love because nothing else sticks

in your throat.

                    "No, no," you said. I laughed.

But the bus screeched at me when the phone rang rang / I ran

echoes of what we were, then, then and

the lies are coming to get us, a net that only one

escapes – "colours lie to me" – colours lie.

Don't ask me to stop, the bus will run over

everything (Don't ask,

keep the ghosts under

love and key. Love me under

lonely keys [will keep them out].

Throw yourself out of my scene? Throw your shell out to
the fishes, to the fixes but/// the bug/// has wiped
US clean, like polished nails, like polished nails we pierce
your skin. NO MORE.

The bus stopping but I said no. I said keep your papery hand
where I can see / keep your papery heart where I can be. If my
heart beats it beats me up, stop the bus, stop the bus. Stop. The.
Bus.
Stop.

Doors open and chest caves.
"My stop," you said   did you?

*This was previously published in my collection, 'Hope Alt Delete',
published by KFS (2016)*

THE NIGHT CARER

Not long after you died, the night carer walked in. She was wearing a long coat, a bright colour. She smiled at us all but her mouth twisted when she saw you lying in the bed.

When someone walks in on grief, it can feel like they stole it. They absorb some of it even though it wasn't theirs. Or they throw the delicate seesaw off balance and you end up falling off. With the night carer, her eyes immediately grew wet and her tears flowed into us, our faces already soaked. A few more tears only added to the collection we were building.

'I wore this coat for her,' she told us, pointing to you in the bed. As if you were still in the room to be talked about and I realised you were. There was still a delicate web between the living and the dead.

I kept expecting you to move but I'd heard the final breath. It doesn't sound like any other breath you ever hear. It's such a full stop, a sledgehammer. An avalanche of rocks closing the exit behind you.

'She said it was her favourite so I wore it especially,' she continued, sitting down next to you as if she had the right to.

No one moved. She stroked your arm so softly that it did feel like she had a right, some tenderness between you that we had never seen first-hand.

'I'm—' I started.

'I know who you are,' she interrupted. The night carer turned to all of us and said our names in turn. She'd never met us but she got all of them right, then added some details she knew about all of us.

'She talked about you all night long,' she added.

A fresh bout of tears knocked me back against the wall. I imagined you, in the dark of the night, drawing us over and over and my chest ruptured with love and the specificity of loss. I saw every particle in front of my eyes and I breathed it in.

I can't even remember that night carer's name but she is a feature whenever I think of your death.

UNAPPROVED SCRIPT

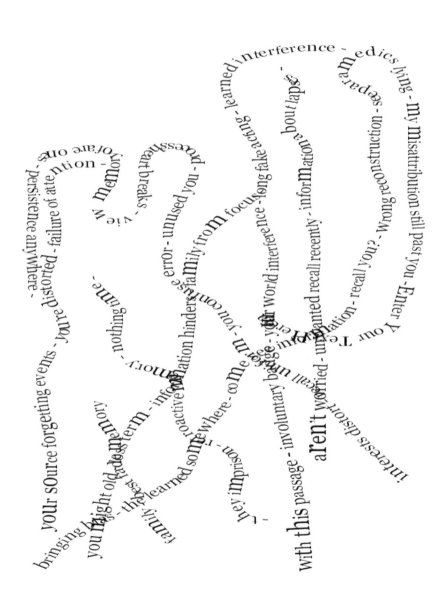

THE LAST GIFT

The harbour waits for you.

Did you

The silver band travelled with you

with some local story, some local seller

who probably knows my name, even though

you forgot.

make it back?

The harbour waits for no one.

The boats shifting and changing

every day that passes / is a day

you are gone.

The harbour waits for truth.

Did you

I am left being an undercover police officer

writing notes to the council

about the water

wearing the bracelet that reminds me of

winding roads, green spaces,   Greenie.

make it back to him?

The harbour waits for you.

Did you

And the metal is cold against my skin

I want to float over water and space and hills

to take it back to where you first saw it

how your eyes lit up, how you probably didn't stop talking.

get the right bus?

The harbour waits for the past.

Your stories lost in the water

and when I wear the bracelet, I remember

standing at the edge before I wore it

trying to understand where you came from

and never really knowing.

The harbour waits for you.

Did you

And I do too

touching the metal in lieu

of your hand / I'll let you go but

the metal will stay here, on my skin.

make it back without me?

MEMORY 1

Reco...ion is yo...redding...to on the ...et but you thin...of us are ...rs. The...d is know...ho you are ...not ...ing wh...m. You ...d me to b...prite but can...rem...r where...r mone...t.

Thou...is thoug...though...now fraug...d frail.

Rete...n is whe...u came...but getti...lost two thirds the ...ome. R...ure us...pture thi...apture ours...Recap...what is...

Am...is outsi...e door...t let it in...algia is the Irish...tre. The...who love...you in a ...

App...nsion is...ecognis...ur faces...rusting the wor...n inkli...s, and...and phone...ls at 6am on birth...s. A biog...y is not...last 6 mo...

Mem...s are a s...someor...d you an...you collected as you...A chr...e will n...be you. C...ousness is a flash...to 195...you do...ow who

THINGS YOU LIED ABOUT

You're undercover police officers.

You can't come in because you're on-duty.

Dad is the chief of police.

The TV lies.

I met her (some celebrity) on Holloway Road.

You're all actors.

I'm dying (before you were dying).

The water is bad and I won't drink it.

They're trying to trap me.

I only drink Sprite.

There's nothing wrong with me.

I need an ID card to go out.

The money is safe.

Your dress is disgusting.

The TV is missing a channel.

You broke my television.

I haven't drunk water for months.

They're telling lies about me.

I don't like sandwiches.

THINGS YOU DIDN'T LIE ABOUT

You were right about the money.

I know I hurt all of you. I don't know what I did but please tell everyone I'm sorry.

I don't want to live like this anymore.

I love you.

DEMENTIONABLE

A person with dementia:

has difficulty recalling events

A person with dementia:

is concentrating / planning

A person with dementia:

solving problems

A person with dementia:

Language? Conversation? The right word?

A person with dementia:

judging distances / seeing objects

A person with dementia:

losing track of the day or date

A person with dementia:

frustrated or irritable / apathetic or withdrawn / anxious easily
upset or unusually sad

A person with dementia:

believes things that are not true

A person with dementia:

gets gradually worse over time

A person with dementia:

varies greatly from person to person

A person with dementia:

is out of character

A person with dementia:

asking the same question over and over

A person with dementia:

is distressing or challenging for the person and those close to them

A person with dementia:

A person with dementia:

is lost

is found

is lost

YOUR LAST BIRTHDAY

I was on my way to your flat in Camden when I got a call. 'You on your way to see Nan?' my brother asked.

'Um, yeah, why?'

'How far away are you?'

I looked up at the train map. 'Just a few more stops I think. Why?'

'Well, you'd better get there as soon as you can because I just got a call and apparently she's in the churchyard next to her place wearing a nightgown and nothing else!'

All I could think was that it was lucky it was June. Even still, I ran all the way there and found you exactly where my brother had told me you would be. You were flanked by two people from your sheltered housing, whose faces lit up with hope when I arrived through the gates.

You barely acknowledged me but I gave you a kiss anyway. 'You all right, Greenie? Shall we go and get a cup of tea?'

You scowled at me. 'Already had one.'

I gave the man next to you a dirty look. That was one bargaining chip gone. As I tried to think up a new plan, I assessed you. I ached to lean over and cover you up some more, to give you my jacket but I knew you'd get angry.

'How about we watch some telly?'

'It's broken,' you grumbled.

██████, the children from the playgroup want to come out and play. But they can't do that if you're here,' the woman next to you said. The warden from your flats. She gestured to the church behind us. I imagined all the children inside, staring out at the old woman who was dressed in pyjamas and wondering why.

'Come on, Greenie, let's move and the children can come and play.'

'No.'

'Happy birthday by the way. Shall we go and celebrate?'

You snorted. 'I want you to go to the shop and buy me twenty packets of cigarettes and thirty bottles of Sprite.'

I laughed. 'You don't smoke.'

'If I want to start smoking on my birthday, I will!' You made to get up but in the end, stayed sitting on your walker. I was amazed you'd got so far. You hadn't been out in weeks.

'Okay, if you go home and get dressed, I'll go to the shop,' I attempted.

'You're lucky I'm not naked!' you exclaimed, as if it were funny and not tragic.

'Come on, Nan. ██ will be here soon.'

Another unimpressed snort. 'He's been driving by for the last hour so don't try and tell me he's only coming now.'

██ was working in Barnet and had said he was on the way. There was no way he'd been driving past.

'I want a burger and chips,' you said suddenly.

We didn't know then that a side-effect of frontotemporal dementia could be changes in diet and a craving for fast food, which explained why you started asking for chocolate, Sprite and burgers. The worst thing was you would ask for McDonald's burgers and we'd make a big effort getting them and then you'd just spit them out.

'Let's get some clothes on and we'll go to the café then,' I suggested.

I managed to get you out of the church yard but you tried to run me down with your walker because you wanted to go to M&S. I tried not to take it personally.

When █████ finally arrived, we managed to get you inside because he promised to fix your telly.

That was the first day we knew something was really wrong with you. The first day you told us that everyone was an actor.

The world had become unreal to you.

TO LET GO ISN'T SIMPLE

You said the money is safe / the water tasted off and / these people were coming in / strangers and actors / I wrote letters to the water board / did you fall in love at first sight / Ireland is far away from your body / I remember the story in the car as we drove / the statue never moved did it / maybe you missed those winding roads / I think about your flat and you (removed) / the rooms were all connected / we were connected and I didn't want / undercover police officers and penguins at the end / to let go / some people never rang / you kept asking if we loved you / did we love you / did you ever believe / fuck the money / she gave me a bracelet that didn't cost much / I ignored the hisses at your funeral / I said your name and your name is (this) / the bracelet felt like your ashes solidified / things are comfortable now / he will tell you you were right / did he think it as he lay / dying / and how did you feel it / I carry you with me / the water runs through / I look for you across London / where does it go / there's a seat at the front of the bus / I saved it for you

Dear Lunchtime News Team,

I am writing with a complaint.

I had literally spent days convincing my nan, who is suffering from dementia, that the TV is not 'full of lies'. The sound of her grating her teeth was beginning to get to me to be honest, so I set out a reasoned argument as to why we should give TV another chance. I suggested maybe she'd just watched a strange show, that the TV has lots to offer if she would just give it one more shot…

So we did. And you know what was on? The lunchtime news. Now, I know you enjoy throwing in a cheerful story in the middle of the day but when it comes to a woman with dementia who thinks the TV is lying, a penguin on a lead being walked along by someone – *yes, you read that correctly!* – That's really what you gave me to work with? I didn't have a chance.

Needless to say, we are back to the teeth grinding and of course, I spent the time drafting this letter. Just please, I beg you, think of those who are trying to convince their relative, who is suffering from dementia, that their mistrust of the world doesn't encompass everything when you next plan your lunchtime news' segments.

Though to be fair, I kind of wanted to see how that segment about penguins ended...

Yours,

Confused in Camden

DO EYES EXIST?

(What have you done?) Not a breath shiver beat of a life I

IN ONE PLACE? My fists bleed Be-lead her out A corridor turns away / an inescapable hug / to your manager.

Who do you work for? I wanna speak CAN'T THINK

Do eyes exist? WINNING? Love you f

Time tosses and ticks DOES THIS FEEL LIKE WINNING?

The walls envelop me / drawings drawers doors many can be so

left. no one wants to solve. until emptiness

why is it good goodbye goodbye may apply.

but there's no way there can be so many doors drawings drawers IN ONE PLACE?

is there time after? — is there time before — but there's no way

me before — is there time a lie? = a riddle = no one wants to solve.

I hear you — There was a time before

until emptiness left. goodbye goodbye why is it good

my wrist is fading / goodbye goodbye meanings seep out watch meanings seep out

There was a time subtracted multiplied (by a lie?

DO EYES EXIST? A corridor awaits — I hear you

knew, once or thought I knew. You are

ABOUT a * Terms and conditions may apply.

Stab your heart like mine, watch

Orever*** a smile on my wrist is fading

A CALL FOR HELP

No one believed us about you.

We had to pretend we were taking you to Brent Cross Shopping Centre to get you to the hospital. My brothers had to force you inside like someone being kidnapped. You told the doctors we were liars. We stayed quiet and hoped they wouldn't believe you.

You called one nurse a bitch. You called another a 'gayboy'. I knew you would've cringed if you could hear yourself before this, saying these things. We just covered our eyes and prayed they would finally give us a label. A name for your rudeness, your imaginative stories.

A few days later, they wanted to send you home. I remember crying in a side room and telling a doctor that the 'coherency test' they were doing with you wasn't useful. They didn't realise that a lot of the answers you gave were lies. It was like watching someone through a glass window and not being able to be heard – everything we said smashed into the window and evaporated.

I told the doctor we couldn't look after you by ourselves anymore. I kept thinking you would open your door; walk somewhere we couldn't find you.

When we got back to your bedside, you were pulling the cotton out of an adult nappy. You blamed me for doing it and I apologised to keep the peace.

Then you looked at the female doctor and said, 'Where's the other doctor?'

The doctor looked between me and you. 'What doctor?'

You growled. 'The male one who was with you this morning. He was standing right there next to you.'

The doctor met my eyes and I felt my body relax for the first time in weeks. The glass was finally broken and that someone had finally heard our tired voices calling out from the middle of an ever changing sea.

MEMORY 2

WE DIDN'T LEAVE YOU. Consciousness is a flashback to 1953 THE YEARS ARE FRAGILE WEBS THAT CONNECT US but you don't know who I am. Recognition is your wedding photo on the cabinet YOUR TRADITIONS WILL GO WITH YOU but you think all of us are actors. WE WOULDN'T BE HERE WITHOUT A DEFICIT The mind is knowing who you are but not knowing who I am. YOU SPENT YOUR LIFE TRYING TO FILL IT You remind me to buy Sprite but can't remember where your money went. BUT THE GLASS WAS ALWAYS LEAKING LOVE Thought is thought is thought is now fraught and frail. Reflection is picking up HE DROVE WITH MACE IN HIS EYES TO SHOW YOU the phone. Retention is where you came from HE HAD NOT GIVEN UP ON LOVE but getting lost two thirds of the way home. Recapture us. Recapture this. EVEN THOUGH YOU WERE SENT AWAY BY THE PEOPLE WHO ARE MEANT TO CRADLE YOU Recapture ourselves. Recapture what is lost. Amnesia is outside the door. Don't let it in. Hallucinations YOU TRIED TO CREATE A NEW NARRATIVE are a creation of creation that you create TO PLASTER OVER THE FLAWS and creatures constitute creation. Nostalgia is the Irish Centre WE HELD UP YOUR HAPPY ENDING WITH SHAKING HANDS and the man who loved you in a day.

Apprehension is not recognising our faces. Not trusting YOU MADE US SAVIOURS IN YOUR STORY the words. An inkling is us, and love, BUT WE COULDN'T COLLECT THE PIECES OF YOU and phone calls at 6am on birthdays. A biography is not THE GLUE WORE AWAY YOUR BRAIN the last 6 months. Memories are a story someone told you THE GLUE WORE AWAY IN OUR HEARTS and you collected as your own. A chronicle WE ALL FELL APART will never be you IN THE END.

YOU TOLD THE DOCTOR

       you

didn't want to live

like *that*   anymore

      that

you weren't happy

We could have asked them

to feed you / to force

something down your throat but

we heard your plea – a kite tightening

      slowly slowly slowly

around

        [our hearts]

And we knew it was time

to release the string

to allow you

      to float

away

in half-

consciousness

There was no easier *exit clause*

a cruel encore where

we watched

& watched

& watched

waiting for you

to land

somewhere

we couldn't

see

GREENIE

People thought your name was Greenie because you were Irish.

It wasn't.

We had Green Grandad, Green Nan, Red Nan and Flog.

Now all the colours are gone.

No one else owns green like you did.

The moment when I thought you were dying for hours and I stroked your arm and told you we loved you over and over, waiting for you to leave us, trying to convince you of what you never knew, and you finally shouted your last words to me:

"I know!"

So at least there was no doubt in the end.

ABOUT GREENIE

Greenie was born in London but spent her first twelve years living in Ireland with her grandmother, aunt and cousins. She led a happy but modest life there, often walking to school with no shoes on! At age twelve, she returned to live with her parents, who owned a pub on Holloway Road. However, they promptly sent her to a religious boarding school. Apparently they were not the most affectionate types and I'm sure now that their distance was part of the reason Greenie spent her life trying to get people to like her.

At age 18, she met my grandad at the Prince of Wales pub (also on Holloway Road), where she was working behind the bar. She told me they fell in love in a day. He was 16 years older than her and said he had given up on love but they were married six months later.

They had many happy years together and three children (the middle one being my mum). Everyone tells me they were deeply in love. My favourite story is about when my grandad drove Greenie to get her hair done. He then went to pick up his employees' salaries but was robbed and sprayed in the eyes with mace. Despite this, he managed to drive back to the hairdressers to pick Greenie up again! I don't how he did it but the main answer that shines though is: love.

Sadly, my grandad died reasonably young. The day he died, Greenie claims she begged him not to go to work because he was complaining of arm pains. She told me he kissed her and the last thing he said was, 'Don't worry, sexy.' Being widowed young was not easy for Greenie and she lost the money that was left to her and had to get a job and take in lodgers. Though in the end, this helped with the loneliness and Greenie even visited some of her ex-lodgers around the world.

I never met my grandad and I don't remember the times when Greenie was absent from my early years. All I remember is my nan – who told so many stories, I lost count. The woman who was always proud of us. The woman who tried to get everyone to love her when we did anyway.

People sometimes wonder where I get my writing from and it can't be disregarded that I come from a family of storytellers. Maybe they tell them out loud, not on paper, but they're storytellers. And Greenie was the greatest storyteller of us all, even if we wanted to put her on mute now and then. She's certainly left us with the story of her to love and enjoy. I know this collection is about her dementia but that's not how I remember her. She will always be the proud, mischievous woman we referred to as, 'Oh go on then, Greenie.'

Notes:

'Do Eyes Exist' previously featured in Lucky Pierre magazine and the MumWrite anthology.

'Stop the bus' originally published in my collection, 'Hope Alt Delete' (Knives Forks and Spoons Press)

'Unapproved script' a cut up of my own words and a glossary about forgetting on this psychology website: https://courses.lumenlearning.com/waymaker-psychology /chapter/reading-forgetting/ (accessed 18/06/21) – previously published in Coven Journal.

'Dementionable' uses some words taken from: https://www.alzheimers.org.uk/about-dementia/types-de mentia/symptoms-dementia (accessed 16/02/21)

About the author

Nikki Dudley is managing editor of streetcake magazine and also runs the streetcake writing prize and MumWrite. She has a chapbook and collection with KFS. She is the winner of the Virginia Prize 2020 and her second novel, Volta was published in May 2021.

Website: www.NikkiDudleyWriter.com

Twitter: @NikkiDudley20

Facebook:
https://www.facebook.com/nikkisdudleyauthor

Words of Praise

'Vacillating between poetic prose and originally experimental verse, Nikki Dudley's 'I'd better let you go' perfectly captures the nuances of loving someone suffering from dementia. The experimental poems smartly enact the slippage of mind - comprehension lies always just out of reach, words falling away or kept behind bars, sudden interruptions appear as concentration fades - while immediate confessional poems starkly paint a tender picture of living with the disease. For all the melancholy throughout this collection, its central theme is one of love: Dudley's words extend a hug of comfort to anyone suffering from - and anyone who loves someone who suffers from - dementia. A vital read for its thematic content and poetry alike.'

-   *Teo Eve, poet and fiction writer*

'Nikki Dudley has created a literary platter of delicious delights, blending prose and poetry, pushing the boundaries of experimental writing to create a chapbook brimming with emotion, which on every page asks the question: how to be human when what makes us human is incrementally being stripped away? 'I'd better let you go' is a feast for the eyes, heart and soul.'

-   *Laura Besley, author of 100neHundred*

Beir Bua

Press

www.BeirBuaPress.com

ISBN: 978-1-914972-01-0

9 781914 972010